HÄGAR NORSE CODE

There may be some argument about which European first discovered America—an Italian or a Viking. But now the whole world has discovered that jolly Viking, Hägar the Horrible.

Hägar is back with his entire Viking crew plus Helga, Honi, Hamlet, Snert, Kvack and, of course, Lucky Eddie, Hägar's sidekick.

Here's your chance to join the more than 100 million people who "discover" and enjoy Hägar every day, in over 1600 newspapers around the world.

Hägar's creator is Dik Browne, twice winner of the Ruben Award, the National Cartoonist Society's highest honor.

Hägar the Horrible Books

HÄGAR
The Horrible
NORSE CODE
by DiK BROWNE

CHARTER BOOKS, NEW YORK

HÄGAR THE HORRIBLE: NORSE CODE

A Charter Book / published by arrangement with
King Features Syndicate, Inc.

PRINTING HISTORY
Charter edition / May 1986

ISBN: 0-441-31467-8

Charter Books are published by The Berkley Publishing Group,
200 Madison Avenue, New York, New York 10016.
PRINTED IN THE UNITED STATES OF AMERICA

11-6

DIK BROWNE

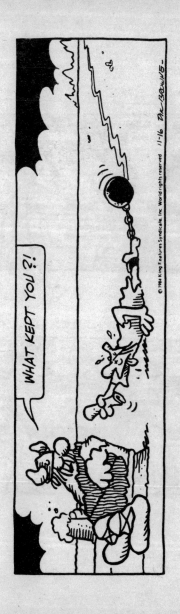